LPIC-3 304-200 Linux Virtualization and High Availability Exam Practice Questions & Dumps

Exam Practice Questions For LPIC-3 304-200
Exam Prep LATEST VERSION

PRESENTED BY: Quantic Books

About Quantic Books:

Quantic Books is a publishing house based in Princeton, New Jersey, USA. , a platform that is accessible online as well as locally, which gives power to educational content, erudite collection, poetry & many other book genres. We make it easy for writers & authors to get their books designed, published, promoted, and sell professionally on worldwide scale with eBook + Print distribution. Quantic Books is now distributing books worldwide.

Note: Find answers of the questions at the last of the book.

Sections
1. Virtualization
2. High Availability Cluster Management
3. High Availability Cluster Storage

QUESTION 1

When transferring a physical machine to a full virtualized machine, which of the given properties must be anticipated to adjust from the viewpoint of the guest operating system? (Select TWO accurate answers.)

A. The user accounts within the guest operating system.
B. The properties of the CPU and other hardware devices.
C. The MAC address of the network interfaces.
D. The version of the guest operating system.
E. The software and applications installed on the guest system.

Section: Virtualization Explanation

QUESTION 2

Which of the given reports are correct concerning IaaS computing cases? (Select TWO accurate answers.)

A. Making of new cases can be automated by using scripts or APIs and service interfaces.
B. The root file system of a computing case is at all times defined and can be accessed after the case is destroyed.
C. Each and every user of an IaaS cloud has precisely one computing case.
D. Once made, computing cases are rarely deleted in order to guarantee the accessibility of the case's data.
E. Cases may be made when needed and destroyed when they become outdated.

Section: Virtualization Explanation

QUESTION 3

Which of the given technologies is the most significant
element of IaaS clouds?

A. Database replication
B. DNS delegation
C. Emulation
D. Mandatory Access Control
E. Virtualization

Section: Virtualization Explanation

QUESTION 4

Which of the given reports are correct concerning Xen
domains? (Select TWO accurate answers.)

A. Fully virtualized and paravirtualized domains are achieved
using the same tools and commands.
B. Xen domains of all kinds need virtualization extensions in
the host system's CPU.
C. All fully virtualized domains are termed 'Dom0' while all
paravirtualized domains are termed 'DomU'.
D. Both paravirtualized and fully virtualized domains may run
on the same host system.
E. Paravirtualized domains are significantly slower than fully
virtualized domains.

Section: Virtualization Explanation

QUESTION 5

Which of the given directives is used in the configuration file of a Xen guest domain in order to define network interfaces?

A. vif
B. eth
C. vnet
D. vbr
E. net

Section: Virtualization Explanation

QUESTION 6

Which of the given tools is used to cooperate with XenStore?

A. xenstore-ls
B. xendo
C. xs
D. xl store
E. xstore

Section: Virtualization Explanation

QUESTION 7

Which of the given KVM parameters is undistinguishable to the KVM parameter -hdb file.img?

A. -drive bus=ide1,type=slave,image=file.img
B. -drive image=file.img,if=ide,device=hdb
C. -drive bus=hd,busid=b,src=file.img
D. -drive file=file.img,index=1,media=disk,if=ide
E. -drive type=loop,src=file.img,dst=disk:hdb

Section: Virtualization

QUESTION 8

When used with KVM, which of the given block device image arrangements support snapshots?

A. qcow
B. dmg
C. qed
D. qcow2
E. raw

Section: Virtualization Explanation

QUESTION 9

Within the graphical output of a KVM virtual machine, which key order switches to the KVM monitor of the VM?

A. Ctrl-Alt-1
B. Ctrl-Alt-0
C. Ctrl-Alt-4
D. Ctrl-Alt-2
E. Ctrl-Alt-3

Section: Virtualization Explanation

QUESTION 10

Which of the given tasks is done by Vagrant?

A. It transfers virtual machines automatically among host systems to circulate the load of all virtual machines equally to all hosts involved.
B. It automates the installation of a virtual machine according to a configuration file describing the desired VM.
C. It monitors the functionality of a virtual machine and restarts the VM if of failure.
D. It is a hypervisor optimized for the usage in embedded systems based on the ARM CPU architecture.
E. It is a programming interface used to create reports from collected performance and resource usage data of a libvirt-based virtualization infrastructure.

Section: Virtualization Explanation

QUESTION 11

Which of the given commands given a detailed list of all image files contained in the libvirt storage pool vol1?

A. virsh list --volumes --pool vol1 --details
B. virsh vol-details vol1
C. virsh --show-pool vol1 --details
D. virsh vol-list vol1 --details
E. virsh volumes --source vol1 –details

Section: Virtualization Explanation

QUESTION 12

When making a public machine image for the provisioning of new cloud computing cases, which of the given steps must be done? (Select TWO accurate answers.)

A. Eradicate all default users and groups, involving root and nobody.
B. Eradicate all configuration files from /etc/ that were not manually modified.
C. Eradicate all confidential data from the image.
D. Eradicate all remote login services (i.e. SSH) from the image.
E. Eradicate all private SSH keys from the image.

Section: Virtualization Explanation

QUESTION 13

What is the usual way to gain command line access to computing cases in an IaaS cloud?

A. By giving a public SSH key to the cloud management system and using the matching private SSH key to log into the cases.

B. Typically computing cases are accessed through a web frontend and do not let command line access.

C. By either telnet or SSH using the credentials of the cloud management system account with administrative privileges.

D. By using a telnet session with the credentials set and publicized by the creator of the computing case's system image.

E. By using a VNC console which does not need authentication when it is invoked via the cloud management system.

Section: Virtualization Explanation

QUESTION 14

Which of the given reports are correct for full virtualization?
(Select TWO accurate answers.)

A. Full virtualization does not need variations to the guest
   operating systems.
B. Full virtualization has no performance effect compared to a
   non-virtualized bare-metal installation on the same
   machine.
C. Full virtualization has a severe performance effect and
   must not be used in production environments.
D. Full virtualization may be supported by special CPU
   extensions that give better performance.
E. Full virtualization at all times needs other software elements
   and cannot be done using Linux only.

Section: Virtualization Explanation

QUESTION 15

Which of the given reports are correct concerning hardware based virtualization? (Select TWO accurate answers.)

A. Hardware based virtualization needs special support in the host system's hardware which is present in all recent x86-based computers.
B. Hardware based virtualization implements a whole machine in software and therefore can run virtual machines of a given hardware platform on an arbitrary host system.
C. Hardware based virtualization relies on the host system's processor to call the hypervisor when critical instructions are implemented by a virtual machine.
D. Hardware based virtualization is not accessible on x86-based CPU architectures and needs special virtualization host hardware.

Section: Virtualization Explanation

QUESTION 16

After the Xen guest configuration file debian.cfg has been made and effectively tested, which other action needs to be done in order to make this Xen guest start automatically every time the host system boots?

A. It is essential to add xendomains_auto = yes to the virtual machine configuration file.
B. It is essential to add an entry for debian.cfg to the file /etc/xen/guesttab.
C. It is essential to run the command xl autostart debian.cfg.
D. It is essential to add a symbolic link to the configuration file in the /etc/xen/auto/ directory.
E. It is not possible to use Xen and its tools to start virtual machines automatically.

Section: Virtualization Explanation

QUESTION 17

Which choices to the xl command will deactivate a running Xen virtual machine? (Select TWO accurate answers.)

A. destroy
B. Eradicate
C. shutdown
D. stop
E. halt

Section: Virtualization Explanation

QUESTION 18

Which of the given is correct concerning the CPU of a KVM virtual machine? (Select TWO accurate answers.)

A. Each KVM virtual machine can only have one CPU with one core.
B. KVM virtual machines support numerous virtual CPUs in order to run SMP systems.
C. The CPU architecture of a KVM virtual machine is independent of the host system's architecture.
D. For each KVM virtual machine one dedicated physical CPU core needs to be reserved.
E. KVM uses the concept of virtual CPUs to map the virtual machines to physical CPUs.

Section: Virtualization Explanation

QUESTION 19

Which report is correct concerning the Linux kernel module that needs to be loaded in order to use KVM?

A. It needs to be loaded into the kernel of each virtual machine to give paravirtualization which is needed by KVM.

B. It needs to be loaded into the kernel of the host system in order to use the virtualization extensions of the host system's CPU.

C. It needs to be loaded into the kernel of the host system only if the console of a virtual machine will be connected to a physical console of the host system.

D. It needs to be loaded into the kernel of each virtual machine that will access files and directories from the host system's file system.

E. It needs to be loaded into the kernel of the first virtual machine as it cooperates with the KVM bare metal hypervisor and is needed to trigger the start of other virtual machines.

Section: Virtualization Explanation

QUESTION 20

Which of the given products use container-based virtualization? (Select THREE accurate answers.)

A. KVM
B. Linux VServer
C. LXC
D. OpenVZ
E. Xen

Section: Virtualization Explanation

QUESTION 21

What action does the virsh restore command do?

A. It restores a virtual machine that was stopped by a kernel panic.
B. It restores a virtual machine from a state file.
C. It reverts a virtual machine, involving its storage devices, to a previously saved state.
D. It wakes up a virtual machine that was hibernated by the operating system running inside the virtual machine.

Section: Virtualization

QUESTION 22

How can data be shared among numerous virtual machines running on the same Linux-based host system?

A. By mounting other VM's file systems from /dev/virt-disks/remote/.
B. By using a network file system or file transfer protocol.
C. By default, Linux-based virtualization products give full access to the host system to all virtual machines.
D. By setting up a ramdisk in one virtual machine and mounting it using its UUID in the other VMs.
E. By attaching the same virtual hard disk to all virtual machines and activating EXT4 sharing extensions on it.

Section: Virtualization Explanation

QUESTION 23

Which of the given kinds of guest systems does Xen support?
(Select TWO accurate answers.)

A. Paravirtualized guests (PV)
B. Foreign architecture guests (FA)
C. Fully virtualized guests (HVM)
D. Container virtualized guests (CVM)
E. Emulated guests (EMU)

Section: Virtualization Explanation

QUESTION 24

What is XAPI?

A. An extension of libvirt which adds live migration of virtual servers among arbitrary hypervisors.
B. A ReSTful API which is used by xl to communicate with the Xen hypervisor.
C. The communication interface among a paravirtualized Linux Kernel and the Xen hypervisor.
D. A high level tool chain which given advanced management tools and interfaces for Xen.
E. The internal messaging system within the Xen hypervisor.

Section: Virtualization Explanation

QUESTION 25

Which of the given are lawful KVM parameters? (Select THREE accurate answers.)

A. -drive file=iscsi://user%password@fileserver/iqn.2001-04.com.example/1
B. -drive file=rsync://user%password@fileserver:/tmp/file.iso,media=cdrom,readonly
C. -drive file=ssh://user@host/tmp/file.img
D. -drive file=imap://user:password@mailserver:/INBOX/Wufnc6MjYp@mailgate
E. -drive file=http://user:password@fileserver/pub/linux.iso,media=cdrom,readonly

Section: Virtualization Explanation

QUESTION 26

What is oVirt?

A. An extension to the Linux Kernel used to give container virtualization similar to LXC and OpenVZ.
B. A library that given access to numerous dissimilar virtualization technologies in a common manner.
C. A comprehensive management infrastructure for Linux-based virtualization.
D. An approach used to eliminate the need for virtualization termed Zero-Virt.
E. A Linux-based hypervisor similar to KVM and Xen.

Section: Virtualization Explanation

QUESTION 27

Which of the given resources are directly (i.e. without specialized machine images) accessible to users of an OpenStack cloud? (Select THREE accurate answers.)

A. Database servers to store relational data.
B. Virtual machines for computing tasks.
C. Application servers for immediate deployment with Mono applications.
D. Object storage that is accessed through an API.
E. Block storage devices for defined data storage.

Section: Virtualization Explanation

QUESTION 28

How can data in a computing case in an IaaS cloud be permanently saved and accessed even after the reformation of the computing case? (Select TWO accurate answers.)

A. By saving the data to the memory of the computing case using tmpfs.
B. By saving the data anywhere in the computing case's file system.
C. By saving the data to /cloud/defined/ which is given in all common IaaS clouds.
D. By saving the data to object stores given by a distinct service in the cloud.
E. By saving the data on defined block devices that needs to be explicitly connected to the computing case.

Section: Virtualization Explanation

QUESTION 29

Which of the given reports are correct about container-based virtualization? (Select TWO accurate answers.)

A. All containers run within the operating system kernel of the host system.

B. Dissimilar containers may use dissimilar distributions of the same operating system.

C. Each container runs its own operating system kernel.

D. Container-based virtualization relies on hardware support from the host systems CPU.

E. Linux does not support container-based virtualization for the reason that of missing kernel APIs.

Section: Virtualization Explanation

QUESTION 30

Which of the given reports are correct concerning resource management for full virtualization? (Select TWO accurate answers.)

A. The hypervisor may give fine-grained limits to internal elements of the guest operating system for example the number of processes.
B. Full virtualization cannot pose any limits to virtual machines and at all times assigns the host system's resources in a first-come-first-serve manner.
C. It is up to the virtual machine to use its assigned hardware resources and create, for example, an arbitrary amount of network sockets.
D. The hypervisor given each virtual machine with hardware of a defined capacity that limits the resources of the virtual machine.
E. All processes made within the virtual machines are transparently and equally scheduled in the host system for CPU and I/O usage.

Section: Virtualization Explanation

QUESTION 31

Which of the given reports is correct concerning the given output of xl list:

```
Name      ID Mem VCPUs State Time(s) Domain-0       0
384       1 r          498.7
Debian    2  305  1  --p---- 783.5
Slack     6  64   1  -b ---- 313.6
CentOS    7  512  2  r ------455.1
```

A. It is essential to use the xl command to adjust Slack's state to running.
B. CentOS is the domain which has consumed the most CPU time.
C. The domain with ID 2 uses paravirtualization.
D. Both Debian and Slack need xl commands to start running.
E. Slack is idle or waiting for I/O.

Section: Virtualization Explanation

QUESTION 32

A configuration file for a Xen virtual machine was made with file name slack.cfg within Xen's configuration directory. Which of the given commands starts the virtual machine defined in this configuration file and opens the virtual machine's console on the present command line?

A. xl start slack
B. xl create slack.cfg --show-console
C. xl create slack.cfg
D. xl start slack.cfg -c
E. xl create slack.cfg –c

Section: Virtualization Explanation

QUESTION 33

Which of the given commands can be used to define whether the local machine is capable of running full virtualized Xen guests? (Select TWO accurate answers.)

A. dmesg |grep -i intel|grep -i vt; dmesg |grep -i amd|grep -i v
B. egrep '(vmx|svm)' /proc/cpuinfo
C. xl dmesg | grep -i hvm
D. grep -i "Full Virtualization" /proc/xen
E. grep -i "Full Virtualization" /etc/xen/*

Section: Virtualization Explanation

QUESTION 34

Which of the given reports is correct concerning XenStore?

A. It is a web interface used to give self-service domain provisioning to users with sufficient privileges.
B. It saves the defined configuration of all defined Xen domains and restores them when the host system is started.
C. It manages disk file images on behalf of all virtual machines and given them as virtual devices to guest domains.
D. It stores run time information concerning Xen and its domains using hierarchical namespaces shared among domains.
E. It is a software repository located within the host system used to give software packages to the guest domains.

Section: Virtualization Explanation

QUESTION 35

Which of the given limitations is correct when using KVM with the User Network?

A. Virtual Machines needs to use a SOCKS proxy to connect to the internet.

B. Virtual Machines can communicate with the host system and with other virtual machines using User Network.

C. Virtual Machines can only communicate with other virtual machines but not with the host system.

D. Virtual Machines cannot use ICMP.

E. Virtual Machines are restricted to only use IPv6 and not IPv4.

Section: Virtualization Explanation

QUESTION 36

Which of the given commands are needed to start a private network among two (or more) KVM virtual machines that is not visible to other KVM cases on the same KVM host? (Select THREE accurate answers.)

A. ifconfig
B. brctl
C. tunctl
D. ipconfig
E. ebtables

Section: Virtualization Explanation

QUESTION 37

Which one of the given tools can NOT be used to create virtual machines, involving their configuration in a libvirt-based KVM environment?

A. virt-clone
B. virt-install
C. virt-img
D. virt-manager

Section: Virtualization Explanation

QUESTION 38

Which of the given reports is correct concerning VirtualBox?

A. VirtualBox uses container-based virtualization and can only run virtual machines using the operating system of the host system.
B. VirtualBox can only be run from a graphical desktop environment and not from the text console.
C. VirtualBox given special device drivers for numerous operating systems to enhance the virtual machine's performance.
D. VirtualBox contains a hypervisor that runs autonomously from any other operating system on a bare metal host.
E. VirtualBox is part of the vanilla Linux kernel and does not need any other software installation on recent Linux distributions.

Section: Virtualization Explanation

QUESTION 39

Which command within virsh lists the virtual machines that are accessible on the present host?

A. view
B. show
C. list-vm
D. list
E. list-all

Section: Virtualization Explanation

QUESTION 40

What is the effect of running the virsh vcpupin CLUSNODE-2 4 2 command?

A. It sets the affinity of virtual CPU 4 of virtual machine CLUSNODE-2 to physical processor 2.
B. It reduces the number of virtual CPUs in CLUSNODE-2 from 4 to 2.
C. It increases the number of virtual CPUs in CLUSNODE-2 from 2 to 4.
D. It sets the affinity for all virtual CPUs of virtual machine CLUSNODE-2 to the physical processors 2 and 4.

Section: Virtualization Explanation

QUESTION 41

Which of the given reports is correct concerning a failover cluster?

A. The core element of every failover cluster is a load balancer.
B. Every service may not be run more than once in a cluster.
C. Failover clusters give scalability of a service beyond the capacities of one cluster node.
D. Failover clusters at all times need storage that is shared by all nodes.
E. In normal operation, services may be spread over all nodes.

Section: High Availability Cluster Management

QUESTION 42

Which of the given reports describes fencing resources in a high availability cluster?

A. Fencing is the automated stop and restart of cluster services that suffer from software errors.
B. Fencing is the disconnection of a failed cluster node from any other cluster resources.
C. Fencing is the forwarding of incoming network connections to backend servers.
D. Fencing is the assignment of services to dissimilar cluster nodes to avoid interference of the services.
E. Fencing is the accounting and limitation of disk usage on shared storage.

Section: High Availability Cluster Management

QUESTION 43

If one service in a Pacemaker cluster hangs on another service running on the same node, which score must be assigned to the constraint describing that dependency?

A. -1
B. 0
C. 1
D. FORCE
E. INFINITY

Section: High Availability Cluster Management

QUESTION 44

Which of the given sections are found in the Pacemaker configuration XML file?

A. <pacemaker> and <corosync>
B. <configuration> and <status>
C. <nodes> and <services>
D. <ressources> and <services>
E. <cluster> and <state>

Section: High Availability Cluster Management

QUESTION 45

Which of the given reports are correct concerning the Red Hat Enterprise Linux High Availability Add-On? (Select TWO accurate answers.)

A. It offers support for load balanced clusters only and cannot manage failover clusters.

B. It does not comprise any storage elements.

C. It can be achieved using the regular Pacemaker commands like pcs.

D. It uses its own messaging subsystem, RHMQ, for cluster communication.

E. It is built on top of numerous high obtainability elements that are also accessible in other Linux distributions.

Section: High Availability Cluster Management

QUESTION 46

Using Linux Virtual Server (LVS) without any other tools given which of the given features?

A. Balancing network connections across numerous backend servers.

B. Automatically taking over the services of failed nodes.

C. Restarting failed services on the backend servers.

D. Ensuring the integrity of services on backend servers.

E. Starting and stopping backend servers as needed.

Section: High Availability Cluster Management

QUESTION 47

Which of the given device classes are usually used STONITH devices? (Select THREE accurate answers.)

A. Uninterruptable Power Supplies, UPS
B. CPU frequency management tools
C. Blade Control Devices
D. Remote Management Services like iLO or DRAC
E. Local node storage

Section: High Availability Cluster Management

QUESTION 48

Which actions must be taken in a load balanced cluster in order to protect the load balancer in contradiction of outages?

A. Load balancers cannot be protected in contradiction of outages which is why they must at all times be built on dedicated hardware.
B. No actions are essential as a load balancer cannot become a single point of failure.
C. Two or more load balancers must be deployed as a cascade that passes packets from one to the other.
D. Two load balancers must be deployed as a failover cluster.
E. Load balancers are used for performance and scalability reasons only and cannot be used to archive high availability clusters.

Section: High Availability Cluster Management

QUESTION 49

Which of the given reports are correct concerning the handling of a hardware error in a high availability cluster? (Select THREE accurate answers.)

A. High availability given automatic recovery from software errors only and cannot mitigate hardware issues.
B. After the cluster deals with an error, no manual actions are needed to bring the cluster back to normal operation.
C. Mistaken elements are physically turned off as they are in an indeterminate state.
D. Services are restarted on or redirected to other cluster nodes.
E. The cluster management elements monitor the health of all cluster elements.

Section: High Availability Cluster Management

QUESTION 50
What is the purpose of fencing in a high availability cluster?

A. Prevent failed nodes from interfering with the remaining intact part of the cluster.
B. Guarantee a consistent assignment of all network connections from a client to the same cluster server.
C. Define constraints on which services may run on the same cluster node.
D. Enforce storage quota and other resource limitations for each service given by the cluster.
E. Give multi-tenancy cluster configuration for cloud computing.

Section: High Availability Cluster Management

QUESTION 51

Which of the given reports are correct concerning the purpose of the capacity of a high availability cluster? (Select TWO accurate answers.)

A. The overall capacity of all elements in the cluster doesn't have to be larger than the resources needed in a regular setup.
B. The number of nodes in a cluster has no influence on the availability as long as the sum of the accessible computing resources is equal.
C. Failover clusters can be used to scale a single service beyond the capacity of a single cluster node.
D. In regular cluster operation, not all resources are used.
E. If of the failure of any element, enough resources needs to remain to give all cluster services.

Section: High Availability Cluster Management

QUESTION 52

Which of the given describes a split brain situation in a high availability cluster?
A. Numerous cluster nodes access a shared resource without coordination.
B. Numerous cluster nodes run dissimilar cases of the same services.
C. Incoming network connections are accidentally forwarded to more than one backend server.
D. In place of shared storage, each node uses local storage achieved by itself and replicates with other nodes.
E. In addition to shared storage, each node has local storage that is not shared with other nodes.

Section: High Availability Cluster Management

QUESTION 53

Which of the given commands can be used to safely test and showing Pacemaker configuration shifts? (Select TWO accurate answers.)

A. crm_test
B. crm_simulate
C. crm_dryrun
D. crm_lab
E. crm_shadow

Section: High Availability Cluster Management

QUESTION 54

How does the command to add a new resource to a Pacemaker cluster using crm begin?

A. crm manage cluster
B. crm configure resource
C. crm service add
D. crm configure primitive
E. crm resource new

Section: High Availability Cluster Management

QUESTION 55

When using HAProxy to load balance requests over a set of web servers, what directive is needed in the HAProxy configuration in order to be able to log, on the backend web servers, the IP address of the client making a request?

A. option reverseproxy
B. option forwardfor
C. option clientlog
D. option exposeclient

Section: High Availability Cluster Management

QUESTION 56

Which of the given are lawful load balancing procedures for HAProxy? (Select TWO accurate answers.)

A. defined
B. weightedrr
C. source
D. leastconn
E. destination

Section: High Availability Cluster Management

QUESTION 57

What is correct for a virtual IP address in the context of keepalived? (Select TWO accurate answers.)

A. The distinct IP addresses of all backend servers are termed virtual IP addresses.
B. Every server running kept alive has precisely one virtual IP address and cannot have any other virtual IP addresses.
C. The virtual IP address is the address to which incoming connections are made in order to reach the load balancer.
D. keepalived uses VRRP to guarantee the availability of the virtual IP address.
E. Within the whole LVS cluster achieved by keepalived, the virtual IP address never appears on any network interface.

Section: High Availability Cluster Management

QUESTION 58

Which of the given are tools or services that manage a Linux Virtual Server (LVS) setup? (Select TWO accurate answers.)

A. keepalived
B. ldirectord
C. lvproxy
D. roundrobind
E. vserverd

Section: High Availability Cluster Management

QUESTION 59

When using the gatewaying/direct routing forwarding technique of Linux Virtual Server (LVS), which of the given reports is correct?

A. The default route of all backend servers needs to point to the LVS host.
B. Every backend server needs to accept packets addressed to the IP address of the virtual service.
C. On the backend servers, all packets appear to originate from the IP address of the LVS host.
D. The link layer addresses of all backend servers needs to be involved in the LVS configuration.
E. When using gatewaying/direct routing, only the round robin algorithm is accessible.

Section: High Availability Cluster Management

QUESTION 60

In a Pacemaker cluster, which one of the given commands shows the right syntax for fencing the node on port 3 using the APC rack PDU device which can be found at IP address 192.168.1.145?

A. apc_stonith -a 192.168.1.145 -l apc -n 3 -v -o shutdown -r now
B. fence_apc -a 192.168.1.145 -l apc -p apc -n 3 -v -o shutdown -r now
C. fence_apc -a 192.168.1.145 -l apc -p apc -n 3 -v -o reboot
D. apc_stonith -a 192.168.1.145 -l apc -p apc -n 3 -v -o reboot

Section: High Availability Cluster Management

QUESTION 61

Which of the given are Pacemaker elements? (Select TWO accurate answers.)

A. ccmd
B. crmd
C. fencer
D. pengine
E. keepalived

Section: High Availability Cluster Management

QUESTION 62

Which one of the given is NOT a needed element for running an OCFS2 filesystem resource in a Pacemaker cluster?

A. A clone resource for the OCFS2 file system.
B. A shared storage device accessible by all nodes using the OCFS2 filesystem.
C. The distributed lock manager (DLM).
D. The cluster logical volume manager (CLVM).
E. The O2CB service.

Section: High Availability Cluster Storage Explanation

QUESTION 63

What is the name and path of the configuration file for the O2CB cluster that coordinates the nodes using OCFS2 filesystems?

A. /etc/ocfs2/cluster.conf
B. /etc/ocfs/cluster.conf
C. /etc/ocfs2.conf
D. /etc/cluster.conf

Section: High Availability Cluster Storage Explanation

QUESTION 64

What is the task of the Cluster Logical Volume Manager, CLVM?

A. It parts the cluster nodes into numerous logical groups that are at all times fenced together.
B. It balances incoming TCP connections to a logical service to numerous backend nodes.
C. It makes logical volumes on shared storage accessible to all cluster nodes.
D. It lets numerous nodes to share file system locks in order to access the same files simultaneously.

Section: High Availability Cluster Storage Explanation

QUESTION 65

Which kernel module needs to be loaded to start a RAID-1 like copy of data on two distinct storage devices for a clustered storage solution?

A. rsyncd

B. drbd

C. clraid

D. clmirror

Section: High Availability Cluster Storage Explanation

QUESTION 66

Which of the given reports are correct concerning OCFS2? (Select TWO accurate answers.)

A. OCFS2 is an integral part of Pacemaker and relies on Pacemaker services for functionality.

B. To avoid the need for shared storage, OCFS2 can replicate the content of its filesystems via the network.

C. When using OCFS2 with other cluster software, OCFS2 needs to be integrated into the overall cluster manager to guarantee consistent cluster behaviour.

D. OCFS2 can be used without any other software as it contains its own cluster manager, O2CB.

E. In addition to filesystems, OCFS2 can handle other cluster services for example IP addresses and server daemons.

Section: High Availability Cluster Storage Explanation

QUESTION 67

Which of the given commands can be used to modify properties for example the number of node slots or the label of an existing OCFS2 filesystem?

A. ocfs2.setprops

B. ocfs2tool

C. crm_edit

D. tunefs.ocfs2

E. o2cbtool

Section: High Availability Cluster Storage Explanation

QUESTION 68

In keepalived, what keyword starts the configuration section for one of the failover servers?

A. lvs_server

B. virtual_server

C. vrrp_case

D. vrrp_sync_group

Section: High Availability Cluster Storage Explanation

QUESTION 69

Which configuration setting eventually outlines which server will be the MASTER with keepalived?

A. advert_int
B. state
C. type
D. priority

Section: High Availability Cluster Storage Explanation

QUESTION 70

Which function is not supported in a GFS2 filesystem?

A. repair
B. grow
C. shrink
D. withdraw

Section: High Availability Cluster Storage Explanation

QUESTION 71

When using the user mode network stack with qemu, TCP and UDP connections work fine but ping does not work. Why is this?

A. The Qemu user mode network stack does not implement ICMP.

B. The problem is caused by inaccurate routing.

C. The Qemu user mode network stack blocks all ICMP traffic.

D. The Qemu user mode network stack needs explicit permission for ping to work.

Section: High Availability Cluster Storage Explanation

QUESTION 72

Which one of the given must NOT be used as a lowlevel device for DRBD?

A. A LVM logical volume

B. A physical hard disk

C. A EVMS volume

D. A loop device

Section: High Availability Cluster Storage Explanation

QUESTION 73

When setting up a KVM virtualization host, which one of the given elements is NOT needed?

A. libvirt
B. kvm kernel modules
C. bridgeutils
D. virsh
E. qemu

Section: High Availability Cluster Storage Explanation

QUESTION 74

What is the purpose of the Cluster Configuration System (CCS)?

A. It controls the cluster configuration information file.
B. It fences a dropped node.
C. It controls ACLs for cluster service access.
D. It controls the network topology and settings for the cluster.

Section: High Availability Cluster Storage Explanation

QUESTION 75

Which of the given reports are correct of full virtualization?
(Select THREE accurate answers)

A. Full virtualization has superior I/O performance through the emulated device drivers.
B. Full virtualization is faster than paravirtualization.
C. Full virtualization needs time and system resources for emulation.
D. Full virtualization needs no modification to the Guest OS kernel.
E. Full virtualization works through CPU emulation.

Section: High Availability Cluster Storage Explanation

QUESTION 76

Where are paravirtualized device drivers installed?

A. In the Guest OS
B. In the Host OS
C. Compiled into the hypervisor
D. No special drivers are needed for paravirtualization.

Section: High Availability Cluster Storage Explanation

ANSWERS

1. Correct Answer: BC
2. Correct Answer: AE
3. Correct Answer: E
4. Correct Answer: AD
5. Correct Answer: A
6. Correct Answer: A
7. Correct Answer: A
8. Correct Answer: D
9. Correct Answer: D
10. Correct Answer: B
11. Correct Answer: D
12. Correct Answer: CE
13. Correct Answer: A
14. Correct Answer: AD
15. Correct Answer: AC
16. Correct Answer: D
17. Correct Answer: AC
18. Correct Answer: BE
19. Correct Answer: B
20. Correct Answer: BCD
21. Correct Answer: B
22. Correct Answer: B
23. Correct Answer: AC
24. Correct Answer: D
25. Correct Answer: ACE
26. Correct Answer: C
27. Correct Answer: BDE
28. Correct Answer: DE
29. Correct Answer: AB
30. Correct Answer: CD
31. Correct Answer: E
32. Correct Answer: E
33. Correct Answer: BC
34. Correct Answer: D
35. Correct Answer: D
36. Correct Answer: ABC
37. Correct Answer: C
38. Correct Answer: C
39. Correct Answer: D
40. Correct Answer: A
41. Correct Answer: E

42. Correct Answer: B
43. Correct Answer: E
44. Correct Answer: B
45. Correct Answer: CE
46. Correct Answer: A
47. Correct Answer: ACD
48. Correct Answer: D
49. Correct Answer: CDE
50. Correct Answer: A
51. Correct Answer: DE
52. Correct Answer: A
53. Correct Answer: BE
54. Correct Answer: D
55. Correct Answer: B
56. Correct Answer: CD
57. Correct Answer: CD
58. Correct Answer: AB
59. Correct Answer: B
60. Correct Answer: C
61. Correct Answer: BD
62. Correct Answer: D
63. Correct Answer: A
64. Correct Answer: C
65. Correct Answer: B
66. Correct Answer: CD
67. Correct Answer: D
68. Correct Answer: B
Reference:
https://manpages.debian.org/stretch/keepalived/keepalived.conf.5.en.html
69. Correct Answer: D
Reference:
https://manpages.debian.org/stretch/keepalived/keepalived.conf.5.en.html
70. Correct Answer: C
71. Correct Answer: A
72. Correct Answer: D
73. Correct Answer: D
74. Correct Answer: A
75. Correct Answer: CDE
76. Correct Answer: A